E. E Nickerson

Highway Songs

E. E Nickerson

Highway Songs

ISBN/EAN: 9783743351233

Manufactured in Europe, USA, Canada, Australia, Japa

Cover: Foto ©Thomas Meinert / pixelio.de

Manufactured and distributed by brebook publishing software
(www.brebook.com)

E. E Nickerson

Highway Songs

HIGHWAY SONGS.

FOR

GOSPEL MEETINGS,

CAMP MEETINGS,

FAMILY WORSHIP,

SABBATH SCHOOLS,

LITTLE SOLDIERS,

———◆——

COMPILED BY

Capt. E. E. NICKERSON.

BOSTON, MASS.
P. O. Box, 2579.
1886.

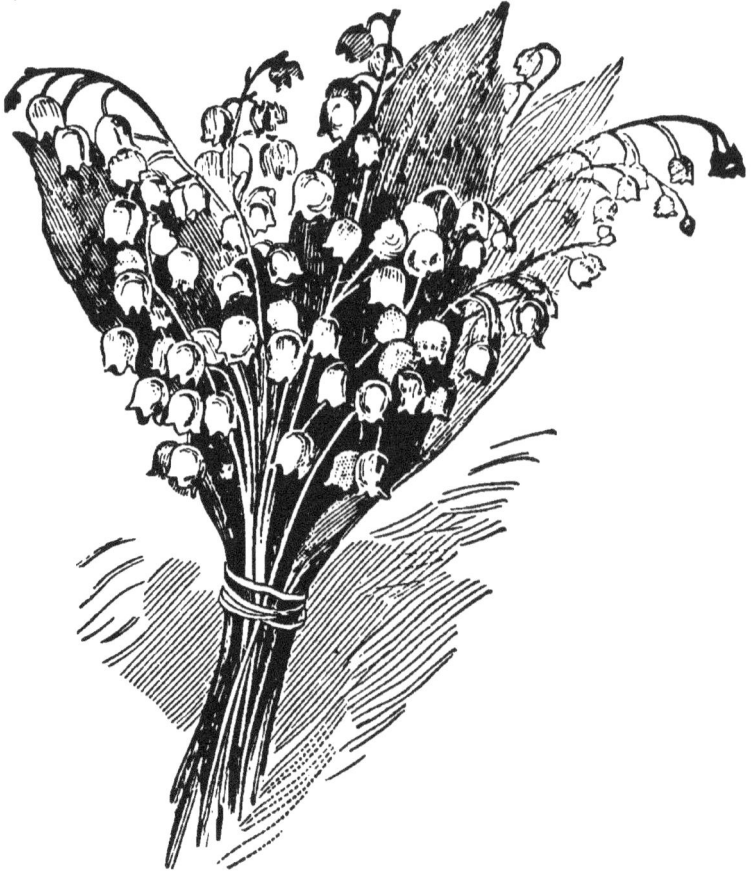

T. H. Lenfest, Music Typographer, School St., Boston.

HIGHWAY SONGS.

1 ## Field of Battle.

E. E. NICKERSON.

1. Come, poor sinner, don't you want to go, Come, poor sinner, don't you want to go,
2. Come, poor drunkard, don't you want to go, Come, poor drunkard, don't you want [to go,
3. Come, backslider, don't you want to go, Come, backslider, don't you want to go,

Yes, all to-geth-er we mean to go, Yes, all to-geth-er me mean to go,

Come, poor sin-ner, don't you want to go And rest in the arms of Je - sus?
Come, poor drunkard, don't you want to go And rest in the arms of Je - sus?
Come, backslider, don't you want to go And rest in the arms of Je - sus?

Yes, all to-geth-er we mean to go And rest in the arms of Je - sus.

CHORUS.

Fighting on the field of battle, Conq'ring on the field of battle, Walking in the light,

Trust-ing in the blood,—Rest-ing in the arms of Je - sus.

2 Companionship with Jesus.

Words by MARY D JAMES.　　　　Music by W. J. KIRKPATRICK. By per.

1. Oh, blessed fellowship divine! Oh, joy supremely sweet! Companionship with Jesus here Makes life with bliss replete: In union with the purest one, I find my heav'n on earth begun.

2. I'm walking close to Jesus' side; So close that I can hear The softest whispers of his love In fellowship so dear, And feel his great Almighty hand Protects me in this hostile land.

3. I'm leaning on his loving breast, Along life's weary way; My path, illumined by his smiles, Grows brighter day by day: No foes, no woes my heart can fear, With my Almighty Friend so near.

4. I know his shelt'ring wings of love Are always o'er me spread; And though the storms may fiercely rage, All calm and free from dread, My peaceful spirit ever sings "I'll trust the covert of thy wings.

REFRAIN.

Oh, wondrous bliss! oh, joy sublime! I've Jesus with me all the time!

Oh, wondrous bliss! oh, joy sublime! I've Jesus with me all the time!

From "SONGS OF TRIUMPH."

3   I Shall Never Know a Sorrow.

As Sung by ADDIE WATERMAN.   E. E. NICKERSON.

1. We are sweeping thro' the land, With the sword of God in hand, We are
2. Oh, the blessed Lord of light, We will serve him with our might, And his
3. We are sweeping on to win Per-fect vic-t'ry o - ver sin, And we'll

watching and we're praying, while we fight; On the wings of love we'll fly, To the
arm shall bring sal-va-tion to the poor; They shall lean upon his breast, Know the
shout our Saviour's praises ev - er-more; When the strife on earth is done, And
(some

souls a - bout to die, And we'll force them to be-hold the precious light!
sweetness of his rest,—Of his pardon he the vilest will as-sure.
mil-lion souls we've won, We'll re-join our conqu'ring comrades gone be-fore.

CHORUS.

O-ver there, o-ver there, I shall never know a sorrow over there: In the
o-ver there, o-ver there, o-ver there,

streets of shining gold, with the glory in my soul, I shall never know a sorrow over there!
over there!

4   'Tis so Sweet to Trust in Jesus.

Words by Mrs. LOUISA M. R. STEAD.   Music by W. J. KIRKPATRICK.   By per.

1. 'Tis so sweet to trust in Je-sus, Just to take him at his word;
2. O, how sweet to trust in Je-sus, Just to trust his cleansing blood;
3. Yes, 'tis sweet to trust in Je-sus, Just from sin and self to cease;
4. I'm so glad I learn'd to trust thee, Precious Je-sus, Saviour, Friend;

Just to rest up-on his promise; Just to know, "Thus saith the Lord."
Just in sim-ple faith to plunge me 'Neath the healing, cleansing flood.
Just from Je-sus sim-ply taking Life, and rest, and joy and peace.
And I know that thou art with me, Wilt be with me to the end.

REFRAIN.

Je-sus, Je-sus, how I trust him; How I've prov'd him o'er and o'er.

Je-sus, Je-sus, Precious Je-sus! O for grace to trust him more.

5 **Memories of Galilee.**

ROBERT MORRIS, L. L. D.   H. R. PALMER.   By permission.

. Each cooing dove,   and sighing bough,   That makes the
2. Each flowing glen,   and mossy dell,   Where happy
3. And when I read   the thrilling love   Of him who

eve   so blest to me,   Has something far   di - vi - ner
birds in song a - gree, Thro' sunny morn   the praises
walk'd up-on the sea,   I long, oh, how   I long once

now,   It bears me back   to Gal - i - lee.
tell   Of sights and sounds   in Gal - i - lee.
more   To fol-low him   in Gal - i - lee.

CHORUS.

1. O, Gal - i - lee, sweet Gal - i - lee, where Je - sus lov'd so much to be;
2. O, Cal - va - ry, dark Cal - va - ry, where Je - sus shed his blood for me;

O, Gal - i - lee, blue Gal - i - lee, Come sing   thy song a-gain to me.
O, Cal - va - ry, dark Cal - va - ry, Speak to   my heart from Cal - va - ry.

6   The Lily of the Valley.

Wm. Fry.   (As Sung by E. E. Nickerson.)   J. P. W.

1. I've found a friend in Jesus, He's everything to me,   He's the fair-est of ten
2. He all my griefs has taken, and all my sorrows borne ; In temptation He's my
3. He'll never, never leave me, nor yet forsake me here, While I live by faith, and

thou-sand to my soul ; The Li - ly of the Valley in Him a-lone I see, All I
strong and mighty tow'r ; I've all for Him forsaken, I've all my i-dols torn From my
do   His blessed will ; A wall of fire about me, I've nothing now to fear ; With His

need to cleanse and make me fully whole ; In sorrow he's my comfort, in trouble he's my
heart, and now he keeps me by his pow'r ; Though all the world forsake me, and Satan
man-na He my hun-gry soul shall fill ; Then sweeping on to glory we see His blessed
[tempts me

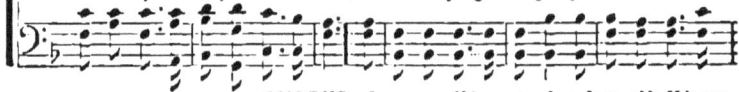

CHORUS.—In sorrow He's my comfort, In trouble He's my

Hallelujah !

stay, He tells me every care on Him to roll. He's the Li - ly of the
sore, Thro' Je-sus I shall safe-ly reach the goal. He's the Li - ly of the
face, Where rivers of de - light shall ev - er flow. He's the Li - ly of the

Valley, the bright and morning Star, He's the fairest of ten thousand to my soul.

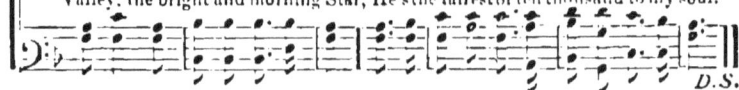

D.S.

7   When the Roll is Called in Heaven.

As Sung by Happy Jennie.   E. K. Nickerson

1. When the roll is call'd in heaven, And the host shall mus-ter there,
2. When the roll is call'd in heaven, I will an - swer to my name,
3. When the roll is call'd in heaven, To the front I'll make my way,

I will take my place among them, And their joys and triumphs share.
And come forward at the summons My in - her - it-ance to claim.
And be welcom'd by the Mas-ter To the realms of end-less day!

CHORUS.

An-gels call the roll up yon - der, Muster day in heav'n pro-claim,

Call the roll, and at the summons I will an - swer to my name.

Tune,—"Silver Threads among the Gold."

1 I had wandered far from Jesus,
   And in sin I went astray;
But my Saviour he had found me,
   And he saves me day by day.
Now I live to please King Jesus,
   He who gave himself for me,
And I'm happy with Salvation,
   And I know he sets me free.
     Chorus.
Come, oh, come to Christ, poor sinner,
   He is waiting to forgive;

He is willing now to save you,
   Come to him and you shall live.

2 Why reject the offered mercy,
   Which the Saviour offers thee?
He has died for your salvation,
   On the Cross of Calvary.
Now, poor sinner, do not linger,
   He has died for you and me!
He will give you full Salvation,
   To the Cross for refuge flee.

Marching On.

Words and Music by Capt. JOHNSON, A.D.C.

1. Marching on in the light of God, Marching on, I am marching on;
2. Marching on thro' the hosts of sin, Marching on, I am marching on;
3. Marching on while the sceptics sneer, Marching on, I am marching on;
4. Marching on with the flag un-furl'd, Marching on, I am marching on;
5. Marching on with the "Blood and Fire," Marching on, I am marching on;

CHORUS.

Up the path that the Master trod, Marching, marching on.   A robe of white, a
Vict'ry's mine while I've Christ within, Marching, marching on.
Per - fect love casteth out all fear, Marching, marching on.
Preaching Christ to the dying world, Marching, marching on.
On till the Lord says "Come up higher," Marching, marching on.

crown of gold, A harp, a home, a man-sion fair, A victor's palm, a

joy un-told, Are mine when I get there: For Jesus is my Saviour, He's

wash'd my sins away, Paid my debt on Calv'ry's mountain; Happy in His dying love,

Sing-ing all the day, I'm liv-ing, yes, I'm liv-ing in the Fountain.

9   Take all my Sins away.

MARECHALE BOOTH.   MARECHALE BOOTH.

1. Oh, spotless Lamb, I come to thee, No long-er can I from thee stay;
2. My hun-gry soul cries out for thee, Come, and for-ev-er seal my breast;
3. Wea-ry I am of in-bred sin, Oh, wilt thou not my soul re-lease?
4. I plunge be-neath thy precious blood, My hand in faith takes hold on thee;

Fine.

Break ev-'ry chain, now set me free, Take all my sins a-way.
To thy dear arms at last I flee, There on-ly can I rest.
En-ter, and speak me pure with-in, Give me thy per-fect peace.
Thy prom-is-es just now I claim, Thou art e-nough for me.

D.S. My precious Sav-iour, full of love, Take all my sins a-way.

CHORUS.   D.S.

Take all my sins a-way, Take all my sins a-way

My Telegram's Gone.

Words by Capt. SAWERS.　　　　　　　　Music by WM. B. BRADBURY.　By per.

1. What wondrous meth-ods God has given! Sal-va-tion wires, from earth to
2. God's tel-e-graph is strong and free, My mes-sage goes with-out a
3. I wire for God my soul to fill, I wire for power to do his
4. I wire to get the Spirit's shower, I wire for full sal-va-tion

heaven; The Spir-it's cur-rents run up there: I'll send a tel-e-
fee; God's image is the stamp I choose, God's pro-mise is the
will; I wire be-fore the throne of grace, I wire to reach the
power; I wire for blood and fire to wave, I wire for God to

CHORUS.

gram of prayer. My tel-e-gram's gone, ... My tel-e-gram's gone, ...
form I use.
ho-ly place.
come and save. My telegram's gone, My telegram's gone,

To the pal-ace of glo-ry my tel-e-gram's gone; My Fa-ther's

there; He'll answer prayer: My telegram's gone, my telegram's gone.

11 I am a Child of a King.

Arr. by Capt. SAWERS.

Not too fast.

1. I am a Christ-ian sol-dier—One of the noi-sy crew;
2. They sing and shout in heav-en—It is their heart's de-light;
3. My sins are all for-giv-en, Which did as mount-ains rise;

Cho.—I am a child of a King, I am, I am a child of a King;

I shout when I am hap-py, And that I mean to do.
I'll shout when I am hap-py, And that with all my might.
My ti-tle's clear for heav-en,—Yon coun-try in the skies.

It is, it is a glo-rious thing To be a child of a King.

Some say I am too noi-sy, I know the rea-son why;
I've Je-sus Christ with-in me,—He's turn'd the dev-il out;
God's saints are my com-pan-ions, I'm bound for end-less day;

I am a child of a King, I am, I am a child of a King;

And if they felt the glo-ry, They'd shout as well as I.
And when I feel the glo-ry, It makes me sing and shout.
And though the storms are rag-ing, I'll sail a-long the way.

It is, it is a glo-rious thing, To be a child of a King

12 Down where the Living Waters flow.

Music by EDWARD E. NICKERSON.

1. Once I was far in sin, But Je - sus took me in,....
2. With Je - sus by my side, I need no oth - er guide,
3. When fight-ing here is o'er, I shall rest for - ev - er - more,

Down where the living wa - ters flow: 'Twas there he gave me sight,
Down where the living wa - ters flow: He is my hope and stay,
Down where the living wa - ters flow: I shall join the blood-wash'd throng,

And let me see the light, Down where the living waters flow.
And He saves me all the way, Down where the living waters flow.
And sing the highway songs, Down where the living waters flow.

CHORUS.

Down where the living waters flow, Down where the tree of life doth grow, I'm

living in the light, for Je-sus now I fight, Down where the living waters flow.

13 Comfort in Affliction.

S. C. Hancock.

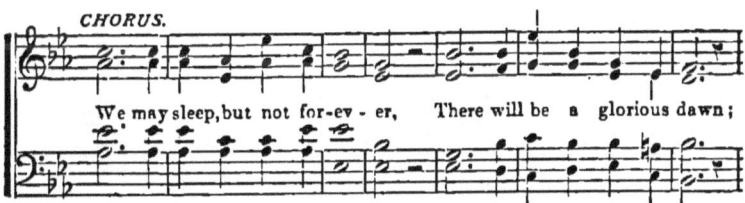

1. We may sleep, but not for-ev - er, There will be a glorious dawn;
2. When we see a precious treasure, That we tend-ed with such care,
1. We may sleep, but not for-ev - er, In the lone and si - lent grave;

We shall meet to part, no, nev - er, On the res - ur - rection morn!
Rudely taken from our bosom, How our aching hearts despair.
Blessed be the Lord, that taketh, Bless - ed be the Lord, that gave.

From the deepest caves of o - cean, From the desert and the plain,
Round its lit - tle grave we lin-ger, Till the setting sun is low,
In that bright E-ter - nal cit - y, Death can nev-er, nev - er come:

From the val-ley and the mountain, Countless throngs shall rise a-gain.
Feel - ing all our hopes have perish'd With the flow'r we cherish'd so.
In his own good time he'll call us From our rest to home, sweet home.

CHORUS.

We may sleep, but not for-ev - er, There will be a glorious dawn;

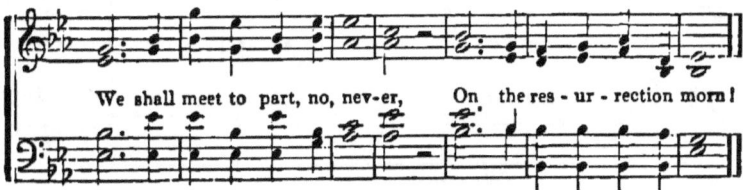

We shall meet to part, no, nev-er, On the res - ur - rection morn!

14   At the Cross.

Sung by ALICE TERRELL.

E. E. NICKERSON.

1. Ere since by faith I saw the stream The bleeding wounds sup-plied,
2. The dy-ing thief re-joic'd to see That fountain in his day,

Re-deem-ing love has been my theme, And shall be till I die.
And there have I, though vile as he, Wash'd all my sins a-way.

CHORUS.

At the cross, at the cross, where I first saw the light, And the

bur-den of my heart roll'd a-way. It was there by

faith I receiv'd my sight, And now I am hap-py night and day!

My Ain Countrie.

15

Miss M. A. Lee.

Scotch Song, Arr.

1. I am far frae my hame, an' I'm wea-ry aftenwhiles, For the
An' I'll ne'er be fu' con-tent un-til my een do see The

D.C. But these sichts an' these soun's will as naething be to me, When I

lang'd-for-hame-bringing, an' my Father's welcome smiles,)
gow-den gates of heav'n, an' my...................... } ain countrie.

hear the angels singing in my........................ain countrie.

Fine.

{ The earth is fleck'd wi' flow-ers, mon-y-tint-ed, fresh and gay; }
{ The bird-ies war-ble blithely, for my Father made them sae; }

D.C.

2

I've his gude word of promise, that some gladsome day the King
To his ain royal palace, his banished hame, will bring
Wi' een, an' wi' heart running owre we shall see
"The King in his beauty," an' our ain countrie.
My sins hae been mony, and my sorrows hae been sair;
But there they'll never vex me, nor be remembered mair,
For his bluid hath made me white, and his hand shall dry my e'e,
When he brings me hame at last to my ain countrie.

3

He is faithfu' that hath promised, an' he'll surely come again,
He'll keep his tryst wi' me, at what hour I dinna ken;
But he bids me still to wait, an' ready aye to be,
To gang at ony moment to my ain countrie
So I'm watching aye, and singing o' my hame as I wait,
For the soun'ing o' his footfa' this side the gowden gate.
God gie his grace to ilk ane wha listens noo to me,
That we a' may gang in gladness to our ain countrie.

16   What Makes Me Happy.

As Sung by JENNIE SMITH.   E. E. NICKERSON.

1. Toss-ing like a troubled o - cean, Tossing like a troubled o - cean,
2. Fill'd with God, we'll shake the Union, Fill'd with God, we'll shake the Union,
3. Now I know what makes me happy, Now I know what makes me happy,
4. Faith triumphant makes it glorious, Faith triumphant makes it glorious,
5. Wash'd in blood, and fill'd with glory, Wash'd in blood, and fill'd with glory,

Toss-ing like a troubled o - cean, Lean-ing on my Saviour's breast.
Fill'd with God, we'll shake the Union, Lean-ing on my Saviour's breast.
Now I know what makes me happy, Lean-ing on my Saviour's breast.
Faith triumphant makes it glo - rious, Lean-ing on my Saviour's breast.
Wash'd in blood, and fill'd with glory, Lean-ing on my Saviour's breast.

THE LION OF JUDAH.

1 'Twas Jesus, my Saviour, who died on the tree,
To open a fountain for sinners like me;
His blood is that fountain, which pardon bestows,
And cleanses the foulest, wherever it flows.

Chorus.
For the Lion of Judah shall break every chain,
And give us the victory again and again;
For the Lion of Judah shall break every chain,
And give us the victory again and again.

2 And when I was willing with all things to part,
He gave me my bounty,—his love in my heart;
So now I am joined with the conquering band
Who are marching to glory, at Jesus' command.

3 And when the last trumpet of judgment shall sound,
And wake all the nations that sleep in the ground,
When heaven and earth shall be melting away,
I'll sing of the blood of the cross in that day.

4 And when with the ransomed by Jesus, my Head,
From fountain to fountain I then shall be led,
I'll fall at his feet and his mercy adore,
And sing of the blood of the cross evermore.

J. P. W.

1. When in the tem-pest he'll hide us, When in the storm he'll be near;
2. When in my sor-row he found me, Found me, and bade me be whole,
3. Why are you doubting and fear-ing, Why are you still un-der sin?
4. You say, "I am weak, I am help-less, I've tried a-gain and a-gain:"

All the way 'long he will car-ry us on,—Now we have nothing to fear.
Turn'd all my night into Heaven-ly light, And from me my burden did roll.
Have you not found that his grace doth abound, He's mighty to save, let him in !
Well, this may be true, but it's not what you do, 'Tis he who's th'"mighty to save."

CHORUS.

Je-sus is strong to de-liv-er, Mighty to save, Mighty to save!

Je-sus is strong to de-liv-er, Je-sus is mighty to save!

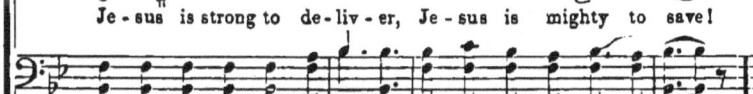

RISEN WITH CHRIST.

1 "Buried with Christ," and raised with
    him too,
What is there left for me to do?
Simply to cease from struggling and strife
Simply to walk in "newness of life."

2 "Risen with Christ," my glorious Head,
Holiness now the pathway I tread;
Beautiful thought while walking therein,
"He that is dead is freed from sin."

3 Liv'ng with Christ, who "dieth no more,"
Following Christ, who goeth before;
I am from bondage utterly freed,
Reckoning self as "dead indeed."

4 Living for Christ, my members I yield
Servants to God, forevermore sealed,
"Not under law," I'm now "under grace,"
Sin is dethroned, and Christ takes its
    place.

Abiding.

Words by CHAS. B. J. ROOT.

Melody by S. C. WRIGHT.

1. A - bid - ing, oh, so wondrous sweet! I'm rest-ing at the Saviour's feet;
2. He speaks, and by his word is giv'n His peace, a rich foretaste of heav'n;
3. I live, not I, through him a - lone, By whom the mighty work is done;
4. Now rest, my heart, the work is done, I'm sav'd thro' the E - ter - nal Son!

I trust in him, I'm sat - is - fied, I'm rest - ing in the cru - ci - fied!
Not as the world he peace doth give, 'Tis thro' this hope my soul shall live.
Dead to my-self, a - live to him, I count all loss his rest to gain.
Let all my pow'rs my soul em-ploy, To tell the world my peace and joy.

CHORUS.

A - bid - - ing, A - bid - - ing, oh, so wondrous sweet!

A-bid-ing in him, Resting in him, oh, so wondrous sweet!

I'm rest - - ing, rest - - ing At the Saviour's feet.

Resting in him, Resting in him,— At the Sav-iour's feet.

19   I Will Follow Jesus.

As Sung by MAUD SCOTT.   E. E. NICKERSON.

1. Down in the val-ley with my Saviour I would go, Where the flow'rs are
2. Down in the val-ley with my Saviour I would go, Where the storms are
3. Down in the val-ley, or up - on the mountain steep, Close be-side my

blooming, and the sweet wa-ters flow; Ev-'ry-where he leads me, I would
sweeping, and the dark wa-ters flow; With his hand to lead me, I will
Sav-iour would my soul ev - er keep; He will lead me safe-ly in the

fol - low, fol - low on, Walk-ing in his footsteps till the crown be won.
nev - er, nev - er fear: Dan-gers can-not fright me if my Lord is near.
path that he has trod, Up to where they gath-er on the hills of God.

CHORUS.

Follow, follow, I will follow Jesus; Anywhere, everywhere, I will follow on:

Follow, follow, I will follow Jesus; Ev'rywhere he leads me I will follow on.

20 Full Salvation.

F. H. STEELE.　　　　　　　　　　　　　　　　　　E. E. NICKERSON.

1. If you want pardon, if you want peace, If you want sighing and sorrow to cease,
2. I am so glad that Jesus sav'd me, Purchas'd my pardon on Calvary's tree!
3. If you want Jesus t' reign in your soul, Plunge in the fountain, and you shall be [whole;

Look up to Jesus, who died on the tree, To purchase a full sal-va-tion.
I am wash'd in th' blood he shed for me there, Enjoying a full sal-va-tion.
Look up to Jesus, who died on the tree, To purchase a full sal-va-tion.

CHORUS.

Liv-ing beneath the shade of the cross, Counting the jewels of earth but dross;

Wash'd in the blood that flow'd from his side, Enjoying a full sal-va-tion.

4 There's peace in believing, sweet peace to the soul,
  To know that he maketh me perfectly whole;
  There's joy everlasting to feel his blood flow,
  'Tis life my Redeemer to know.

5 There's peace in believing, sweet peace to the soul,
  To know that he maketh me perfectly whole;
  Oh, come to the fountain, oh, come at his call,
  There's healing and cleansing for all.

26   Oh! 'tis Glory in My Soul.

Words by FLORA L. BEST.   Music by JNO. R. SWENEY.

1. To thy cross, dear Christ, I'm clinging, All my re - fuge and my plea;
2. Long my heart hath heard thee call-ing, But I thrust a - side thy grace;
3. Love e - ter - nal, light e - ter - nal, Close me safe - ly, sweet-ly in;

Matchless is thy lov-ing kindness, Else it had not stoop'd to me.
Yet, O boundless con-de-scen-sion, Love is shin-ing from thy face.
Sav - iour, let thy balm of heal-ing Ev - er keep me free from sin.

CHORUS.

Oh, 'tis glo - ry! oh, 'tis glo - ry! Oh, 'tis glo - ry in my soul,

For I've touch'd the hem of his garment, And his pow'r doth make me whole.

OH, FOR A HEART TO PRAISE MY GOD.

1 Oh, for a heart to praise my God,
    A heart from sin set free;
    A heart that always feels the blood
    So freely spilt for me.

2 A heart resign'd, submissive, meek,
    My great Redeemer's throne:
    Where only Christ is heard to speak,
    Where Jesus reigns alone:

3 An humble, lowly, contrite heart,
    Believing, true and clean;

Which neither life nor death can part
    From him that dwells within:

4 A heart in every thought renew'd,
    And full of love divine;
    Perfect and right, and pure and good,
    A copy, Lord, of thine.

5 Thy nature, gracious Lord, impart;
    Come quickly from above;
    Write thy new name upon my heart,
    Thy new best name of Love.

27 Away Over Jordan.

As Sung by ALICE TERRELL.   E. E. NICKERSON.

1. Oh, we are go-ing to wear a crown, To wear a star-ry crown.
2. You must re - pent, to wear a crown, To wear a star-ry crown.

Oh, we are go-ing to wear a crown, To wear a star-ry crown.
You must re - pent, to wear a crown, To wear a star-ry crown.

CHORUS.

A - way o - ver Jor-dan, With my bless - ed Je - sus,

A - way o - ver Jor-dan, To wear a star - ry crown.

28   WHEN PEACE LIKE A RIVER.

1 When peace, like a river, attendeth my way,
   When sorrows, like sea billows roll,
   Whatever my lot, thou hast taught me to say—
   It is well, it is well with my soul.
Chorus.—It is well with my soul,
    It is well, it is well with my soul.
2 Though Satan should buffet, though trials should come,
   Let this blest assurance control,
   That Christ hath regarded my helpless estate,
   And hath shed his own blood for my soul.
3 My sin—oh the bliss of this glorious thought—
   My sin—not in part, but the whole.
   Is nailed to his cross, and I bear it no more,
   Praise the Lord, praise the Lord, oh my soul!
4 And Lord, haste the day when the faith shall be sight,
   The clouds be rolled back as a scroll;
   The trump shall resound, and the Lord shall descend,
   "Even so,"—it is well with my soul.

30

My body, soul, and spirit, Jesus, I give
to Thee,
A consecrated offering, Thine evermore to
be.
My all is on the altar, I'm waiting for
the fire.

Cho. Waiting, waiting, I'm waiting
for the fire.

2
O Jesus, mighty Saviour, I trust in Thy
great name,
I look for Thy salvation, Thy promise
now I claim.

3
Oh! let the fire descending just now
upon my soul
Consume my humble offering, and cleanse
and make me whole.

4
I'm thine, O blessed Jesus, washed by
Thy precious blood;
Now seal me by Thy Spirit, a sacrifice
to God.

—o—

31

We're bound for the land of the pure and
the holy,
The home of the happy, the kingdom
of love,
Ye wanderers from God in the broad road
of folly,
Oh, say, will you go to the Eden above?
Will you go, will you go, will you go,
will you go?
Oh, say, will you go to the Eden above?

2
In that blessed land neither sighing nor
anguish
Can breathe in the fields where the
glorified rove,
Ye heart-burdened ones who in misery
languish,
Oh, say, will you go to the Eden above?

3
No poverty there! no, the saints are all
wealthy,
The heirs of His glory, whose nature
is love;
No sickness can reach them, that country
is healthy,
Oh, say, will you go to the Eden above?

4
March on, happy soldiers, the land is before you,
And soon its ten thousand delights we
shall prove;
Yes, soon we'll be massed on the hills of
bright glory,
And drink the pure joys of the Eden
above.

We will go, we will go, we will go, we
will go,
Oh yes, we will go to the Eden above.

You may go, you may go, you may go.

—o—

32

I stand all bewildered with wonder,
And gaze on the ocean of love,
And over its waves to my spirit
Comes peace, like a heavenly dove.

The cross now covers my sins,
The past is under the blood,
I'm trusting in Jesus for all,
My will is the will of my God.

2
I struggled and wrestled to win it,
The blessing that setteth me free;
But when I had ceased from my struggles,
His peace Jesus gave unto me.

3
He laid His hand on me, and healed me,
And bade me be every whit whole;
I touched but the hem of his garment,
And glory came thrilling my soul.

4
The Prince of my Peace is now passing,
The light of his face is on me;
But, listen, beloved, He speaketh—
"My peace I will give unto thee."

—o—

33   TUNE.—"Sweet By and By."

We've a band that shall conquer the foe
If we fight in the strength of the King,
With the Sword of the Spirit we know
We shall sinners to Calvary bring.

Chorus. I believe we shall win,
If we fight in the strength of
the King.

2
We have conquered in times that are
past,
And we've scattered the foe from the
field,
Then we'll fight for the King till the last,
And the Sword of the Spirit we'll
wield.

3
Our foe may be mighty and brave,
And the fighting be hard and severe,
But the King is the mighty to save,
And in conflict He always is near.

2d Cho. I believe "Jesus saves,
And his blood makes me whiter
than snow.

—o—

34

Down at the Cross where my Saviour
died,

Down where for cleansing from sin I
cried;
There to my heart was the blood applied,
Glory to His name!
Chorus. Glory to His name!
Glory to His name!
There to my heart was the blood applied,
Glory to His name!

2

I am so wondrously saved from sin,
Jesus so sweetly abides within;
There at the Cross where He took me in,
Glory to His name!

3

Oh, precious fountain, that saves from
sin,
I am so glad I have entered in;
There Jesus saves me and keeps me clean,
Glory to His name!

4

Come to this fountain, so nice and sweet;
Cast thy poor soul at the Saviour's feet;
Plunge in to-day and be made complete;
Glory to His name!

—o—

35   TUNE.—"Swanee River."

Oh Jesus, how I love to serve Thee;
Filled with thy power
Thy word to me is always precious,
Fulfilled each blessed hour.
One little word when fitly spoken,
Stills all our cares,
That word is peace. the Saviour's token;
It takes away our doubts and fears.

Cho.   All the world leads from my Sav-
iour,
Jesus said 'twas so.
All in Him do find a full salvation.
Sinner, won't you come and go.

2

Dear comrades, pray to be kept watching
For that glorious hour,
When Jesus, at his promised coming,
Shall manifest his raising power;
Then all the saints that sleep in Jesus,
True promise he will raise;
Good Daniel will stand up and greet us
At the ending of the days.

—o—

36   TUNE.—"Tramp, Tramp, Tramp."

O how happy are they who the Saviour
obey,
And have laid up their treasure above;
Tongue can never express the sweet com-
fort and peace
Of a soul that is filled with His love.

Cho.   We'll all shout hallelujah,
As we march along the way,
And we'll sing our Saviour's love,

With the shining host above;
And with Jesus we'll be happy all the
day.

2

That sweet comfort is mine; now the
favor Divine
I have got through the blood of the
Lamb,
With my heart I believe, and what joy I
receive,
What a heaven in Jesus' dear name!

3

Jesus all the day long is my joy and my
song,
Oh that all His salvation might see!
He doth love me I cry, He did suffer and
die,
All to save such a rebel as me.

—o—

37

I'm a happy soldier, on my way to
heaven;
Though in sin I've wandered, I'm for-
given;
When the Saviour saw me on the moun-
tain cold,
He brought the wanderer to His fold.
Free from the bondage, free from the fear,
Crowned with salvation, Heaven right
down here;
Shouting "Hallelujah" as we march
along—
Oh, come and join our happy throng!

2

Since I've joined the army, battles I have
seen;
Conflicts and temptations I've been in;
But the strength of Jesus, daily to me
given,
Has kept me on the way to Heaven.

—o—

1 "Man of sorrows," what a name
For the Son of God, who came
Ruined sinners to reclaim!
Hallelujah! what a Saviour.
2 Bearing shame and scoffing rude,
In my place condemned he stood;
Sealed my pardon with his blood;
Hallelujah! what a Saviour.
3 Guilty, vile, and helpless we;
Spotless Lamb of God was he:
"Full atonement," can it be?
Hallelujah! what a Saviour.
4 Lifted up was he to die.
"It is finished," was his cry;
Now in heaven exalted high:
Hallelujah! what a Saviour.
5 When he comes, our glorious King,
All his ransomed home to bring,
Then anew this song we'll sing:
Hallelujah! what a Saviour.

38   CORONATION.

1 All hail the power of Jesus' name!
   Let angels prostrate fall;
Bring forth the royal diadem,
   And crown him Lord of all.

2 Ye chosen seed of Israel's race,
   Ye ransomed from the fall,
Hail him who saves you by his grace,
   And crown him Lord of all.

3 Sinners, whose love can ne'er forget
   The wormwood and the gall,
Go, spread your trophies at his feet,
   And crown him Lord of all.

4 Let every kindred, every tribe,
   On this terrestrial ball,
To him all majesty ascribe,
   And crown him Lord of all.

5 O that with yonder sacred throng
   We at his feet may fall!
We'll join the everlasting song,
   And crown him Lord of all.

—o—

39

My Saviour suffered on the tree,
   Glory to the bleeding Lamb!
O come and praise the Lord with me,
   Glory to the bleeding Lamb.

The Lamb, the Lamb, the bleeding Lamb.
I love the sound of Jesus' name,
It sets my spirit all in a flame,
Glory to the bleeding Lamb.

2
He bore my sins, and curse, and shame,
And I am saved thro' Jesus' name.

3
I know my sins are all forgiven,
And I am on my way to Heaven.

4
And when the fighting here is o'er
I'll sing upon a happier shore.

5
And this my ceaseless song shall be,
That Jesus tasted death for me.

—o—

40

Return, O wanderer, return,
   And seek your Father's face;
Those new desires which in you burn,
   Were kindled by His grace.
Oh! you must be a lover of the Lord,
Or you can't go to heaven when he comes.

2
Return, O wanderer, return.
   He hears your humble sigh;
He sees your softened spirit mourn,
   When no one else is nigh.

3
Return, O wanderer, return,
   Your Saviour bids you live:
Come to His cross, and you will learn
   How freely He'll forgive.

—o—

41   TUNE.—"Take Back the Heart."

Take back the love thou hast slighted,
   Remember my anguish for thee,
Take back the freedom thou cravest,
   Leaving your sins all with me.
Take back the vows thou hast broken,
   Fulfil them now and be free;
Believe in the word that is written,
   Faith will give freedom to thee.
The signs of the times speak my coming;
   Gaze on the storm cloud and flee,
Resting 'mid strife and confusion,
   Leaving your burdens with me.

2
Come ere the storm overtakes you,
   In love I am pleading for thee;
Come and My Father will meet you,
   Come back a captive to be;
Come back in sadness or sorrow,
   Once more to suffer with me.
I will assure thee thou'rt welcome,
   Gladly I'll then set thee free.
Love shall resume her dominion,
   Striving no more to be free,
When on her world-weary pinion,
   Flies back my lost one to me.

—o—

42   TUNE.—"Robin, Tell Kitty."

I once was a wanderer from Jesus,
   Far away on the mountains of sin;
But now I am housed with the Shepherd,
   His love brought this wanderer in.

Chorus.   Oh sinner, how Jesus does love
      you,
      Just think of the thorns on
       his brow;
      His sweat was like blood in
       the garden,
      To pardon a rebel just now

2
My spirit is free from pollution,
   My heart He has cleansed from all sin.
The saints are my chosen companions,
   And Jesus dwells sweetly within.

—o—

43

Oh, the Lord has borne my sins away.
When the general roll is called, I'll be
   there.
He lives in my heart and has his way.
When the general roll is called, I'll be
   there.
Chorus. I'll be there ready and waiting,

'I'll be there ready and waiting,
I'll be there ready and waiting.
When the general roll is called
I'll be there.

2

Come on, my friends, and go with me.
When the general roll is called, I'll be
there.
I'm bound for glory don't you see.
When the general roll is called, I'll be
there.

3

The devil hates me and I hate him.
When the general roll is called I'll be
there.
He is mad because I don't love sin.
When the general roll is called, I'll be
there.

—o—

44

All for Jesus! All for Jesus!
All my being's ransom'd pow'rs;
All my thoughts and words and doings,
All my days and all my hours.
All for Jesus! All for Jesus!
All my days and all my hours.

2

Let my hands perform His bidding;
Let my feet run in His ways:
Let my eyes see Jesus only;
Let my lips speak forth His praise.
All for Jesus! All for Jesus!
Let my lips speak forth His praise.

3

Since my eyes were fixed on Jesus,
I've lost sight of all beside,—
So enchained my spirit's vision,
Looking at the Crucified.
All for Jesus! All for Jesus!
All for Jesus crucified!

4

Oh, what wonder! how amazing!
Jesus, glorious King of kings,
Deigns to call me His beloved,
Let me rest beneath His wings.
All for Jesus! All for Jesus!
Resting now beneath His wings.
Mary D. James.

—o—

45

1

Jesus, Saviour, pilot me
Over life's tempestuous sea;
Unknown waves before me roll,
Hiding rock and treacherous shoal;
Chart and compass come from Thee,
Jesus Saviour, pilot me.

2

As a mother stills her child
Thou canst hush the ocean wild;

Boisterous waves obey Thy will
When Thou sayest to them, "Be still."
Wondrous Sovereign of the sea,
Jesus, Saviour, pilot me.

3

When at last I near the shore,
And the fearful breakers roar
'Twixt me and the peaceful rest,
Then, while leaning on Thy breast,
May I hear Thee say to me,
"Fear not, I will pilot thee."

—o—

46

Jesus, I my cross have taken,
All to leave and follow thee;
Naked, poor, despised, forsaken,
Thou, from hence, my all shall be:
Perish every fond ambition,
All I've sought, or hoped, or known;
Yet how rich is my condition!
God and heaven are still my own.

2

Let the world despise and leave me,
They have left my Saviour, too;
Human hearts and looks deceive me;
Thou art not, like them, untrue:
And while Thou shalt smile upon me,
God of wisdom, love, and might,
Foes may hate, and friends may scorn me;
Show Thy face and all is bright.

3

Man may trouble and distress me,
'Twill but drive me to thy breast;
Life with trials hard may press me,
Heaven will bring me sweeter rest.
Oh! 'tis not in grief to harm me
While thy love is left to me,
Oh! 'twere not in joy to charm me,
Were that joy unmixed with thee.

—o—

47

Fade, fade each earthly joy,
Jesus is mine!
Break ev'ry tender tie
Jesus is mine!
Dark is the wilderness.
Earth has no resting place,
Jesus alone can bless,
Jesus is mine!

2

Tempt not my soul away,
Jesus is mine!
Here would I ever stay,
Jesus is mine!
Perishing things of clay,
Born but for one brief day,
Pass from my heart away,
Jesus is mine!

Farewell ye dreams of night,
Jesus is mine!
Lost in this dawning bright,
Jesus is mine!
All that my soul has tried,
Left but a dismal void,
Jesus has satisfied,
Jesus is mine!
—o—

48

My life flows on in endless song;
Above earth's lamentation,
I catch the sweet, tho' far-off hymn
That hails a new creation;
Through all the tumult and the strife,
I hear the music ringing;
It finds an echo in my soul—
How can I keep from singing?

2

What though my joys and comforts die?
The Lord, my Saviour, liveth;
What though the darkness gather round?
Songs in the night he giveth:
No storm can shake my inmost calm,
While to that refuge clinging:
Since Christ is Lord of heav'n and earth,
How can I keep from singing?

3

I lift my eyes; the cloud grows thin,
I see the blue above it;
And day by day this pathway smooths,
Since first I learned to love it:
The peace of Christ makes fresh my
heart,
A fountain ever springing;
All things are mine since I am his—
How can I keep from singing?
—o—

49

We may spread our couch with roses,
And sleep thro' the summer day;
But the soul that in sloth reposes,
Is not in the narrow way.
If we follow the chart that is given,
We need not be at a loss,
For the royal way to heaven
Is the royal way of the cross.

2

To one who is rear'd in splendor,
The cross is a heavy load,
And the feet that are soft and tender
Will shrink from the thorny road.
But the chains of the soul must be riven,
And wealth must be as dross,
For the royal way to heaven
Is the royal way of the cross.

3

We say we will walk to-morrow
The path we refuse to-day,
And still with our lukewarm sorrow
We shrink from the narrow way.

What heedeth the chosen eleven
How the fortunes of life might toss,
As they follow'd their Master to Heaven
By the royal way of the cross?
—o—

50

Are you weary, are you heavy-hearted?
Tell it to Jesus, tell it to Jesus.
Are you grieving over joys departed?
Tell it to Jesus alone.
Cho. Tell it to Jesus, tell it to Jesus,
He is a friend that's well-known;
You have no other such a friend or
brother;
Tell it to Jesus alone.

2

Do the tears flow down your cheeks un-
bidden?
Tell it to Jesus, tell it to Jesus.
Have you sins that to man's eyes are hid-
den?
Tell it to Jesus alone.

3

Do you fear the gath'ring clouds of sor-
row?
Tell it to Jesus, tell it to Jesus.
Are you anxious what shall be to-mor-
morrow?
Tell it to Jesus alone.

4

Are you troubled at the tho't of dying?
Tell it to Jesus, tell it to Jesus.
For Christ's coming Kingdom are you
sighing?
Tell it to Jesus alone.
—o—

51

In the rifted Rock I'm resting,
Safely shelter'd I abide.
There no foes nor storms molest me,
While within the cleft I hide.
Refrain. Now I'm resting, sweetly rest-
ing,
In the cleft once made for me;
Jesus, blessed, Rock of Ages,
I will hide myself in Thee.

2

Long pursued by sin and Satan,
Weary, sad, I long'd for rest;
Then I found this heav'nly shelter,
Open'd in my Saviour's breast. *Refr.*

3

Peace, which passeth understanding,
Joy, the world can never give,
Now in Jesus I am finding:
In his smiles of love I live. *Refr.*

4

In the Rifted Rock I'll hide me,
Till the storms of life are past,
All secure in this blest refuge,
Heeding not the fiercest blast. *Refr.*

52   "Ye Would Not."

J. M. S.

Slow.

(Luke 13 : 34.)

J. M. SAWERS.

1. I've knock'd at your heart's door often, I have pled with you o'er and o'er; And the
2. I've knock'd when you were in trouble, I have knock'd when you lay in pain, And you
3. How kind is our Saviour, knocking, When we've lived so long in sin; If you'll

more I'd plead, poor lost one, The firm-er you'd fast-en the door. Ah! your
promis'd sometime you'd open, But that promise was all in vain. Very
knock once more, dear Saviour, I glad-ly will let you in. Ah! you

pleasures will vanish and with-er, Your hopes be blighted and gone; And the
soon life's breath will leave you, Your body sleep 'neath the sod; As he
promis'd, lost soul, once too often, I'm gone from your door ever-more! Oh,

last trump sound from heaven On the Resurrection morn! And the   morn!
knocks, just now, do o - pen, And prepare to meet thy God. As He   God.
Christ! I'm lost for-ev - er, I've to meet an an-gry God! Oh,   God.

CHORUS.

Ye would not, ye would not, ye would not let me in; How

"Ye Would Not." Concluded.

oft I'd redeem'd you from bondage, But ye would not let me in!

rit.

---

53   I'll be with you.

J. M. SAWERS.

1. I am hap-py now in Je-sus, He has wash'd me white as snow;
2. How my soul will leap for glad-ness, When my Je - - sus I will see,
3. When the pearly gates swing o-pen, And the an - - gels' fa-ces see,

Now I'm rest-ing on His promise,— Ev-'ry - where I'll with you go.
And I'll reign with Him for-ev - er, All throughout e - ter - ni - ty!
Then we'll hear our Saviour say - ing, Welcome, child, I died for thee.

CHORUS.

I'll be with you, I'll be with you, Every - where, where'er you go;

Hal - le - lu - jah! I'm re - joicing, For my Sav-iour's voice I know.

Copyright, 1885, by J. M. Sawers.—Used by permission.

54   The Well of Full Salvation.

J. M. S.   (John 4. 14.)   J. M. SAWERS.

1. { What joy in serving Je-sus, It is our heart's delight; We praise him for his
   { His love it is so balmy, His peace it is so sweet, Our ev'ry breath's a

2. { In heav'n we'll see our Je-sus, The blessed Lamb of God, He from our sins re -
   { The world, with all its pleasures, Has sunk beneath our view ; We've laid up

[all our

CHORUS.

goodness, And that with all our might. }
pray-er, In him our joy's com-plete. } We are drinking at the
lieves us ; He is our staff and rod. }
treasures In the land be - yond the blue. }

well of Full Sal-va-tion, Where the Sav - iour gives to all so full and

free,   And he keeps us from the power of all temptation : Won't you

come along and go to heav'n with me?

3 Methinks I hear the chorus,
  Every note so clear and true,
Of the hundred and forty-four thou-
  Oh, what a happy crew! [sand,
All those who love the Saviour,
  Will mingle with that throng,
And praise his name forever
  In everlasting song!

55
Can he come to Jesus?

1. Can a poor sin-ner come to Je-sus? Can he come? can he come?
2. Can a poor drunkard come to Je-sus? Can he come? can he come?
3. Can a back-slid-er come to Je-sus? Can he come? can he come?

Can a poor sin-ner come to Je-sus? Can he come just now?
Can a poor drunkard come to Je-sus? Can he come just now?
Can a back-slid-er come to Je-sus? Can he come just now?

CHORUS.

Yes, oh yes, he can come to Jesus now: While the Saviour now is calling, While the

Holy Spirit's striving, While the precious blood is flowing, He can come just now.

Copyright, 1861, in "Golden Chain," by W. B. Bradbury. Used by per. Biglow & Main.

56
1. Down in the valley, among the sweet grasses,
Walks my Beloved,—his footprints I see;
Haste I to follow him, Saviour and Lover,
How the winds whisper thy dear name to me.
2. Know'st thou I seek thee? O haste to discover
The place of thy shelter'd and fragrant retreat,
Where thou doth rest with thy flocks at the noontide,
By fountains of water, unsearch'd by the heat.
3. Gentler thy voice than the whisper of angels,—
Brighter thy smile than the sun in the sky;
Gather me tenderly close to thy bosom,
Faint with thy loveliness—there let me die!

57   Going Up.

Words as Sung by Liéut. Moore.   E. E. Nickerson.

1. Go-ing up to my purchas'd possession, My friends and companions to meet,
2. Go-ing up to u-nite with the voic-es That like many wa-ters do sound,
3. Going up, for the *Master* hath promis'd, Going up when the trumpet shall sound
4. Go-ing up with a faith calm and steady, My day's work completed at noon;

Where sanc-ti-fied millions are casting Their crowns at Im-man-uel's feet.
My soul in the prospect re-joic-es, With glo-ry I soon shall be crown'd.
With the millions whose bodies now slumber In the sea and un-der the ground.
Go tell ev-'ry one to be read-y, For the Mas-ter is com-ing soon!

CHORUS.

Go-ing up to my purchas'd possession, Go-ing up to my permanent rest;

Go-ing up with the *Ho-ly* pro-ces-sion, Going up at my Saviour's be-hest.

58   The Sanctifying Power.

R. K. C.

R. KELSO CARTER.

1. O glo-ry, hal-le-lu-jah! Sound the joyful strain; Glory to the name of
2. O glo-ry, hal-le-lu-jah! Let the anthem swell; Glory to the name of
3. O glo-ry, hal-le-lu-jah! Let his praises roll; Glory to the name of
4. O glo-ry, hal-le-lu-jah! For the peace within; Glory to the name of

Je - sus! For he par-dons ev-'ry sin, and cleanses ev-'ry stain;
Je - sus! For.. Christ, the Son of God, hath conquer'd death and hell;
Je - sus! For he sends the Ho-ly Ghost, and sanc-ti-fies the soul;
Je - sus! For his strength is form'd in weakness, keeping us from sin;

CHORUS.

Glo-ry to the name of Je-sus!..... Glo-ry, hal-le-lu-jah!

Glo-ry to his name! There's a sanc-ti-fy-ing pow-er in the

blood of Je-sus Christ, A sanc-ti-fy-ing pow-er, hal-le-lu-jah!

59 When we arrive at Home.

T. E. M.

Arr. by J. P. WESTON.

1. My comrades here who love the Lord, And taste the sweets of Jesus' word, In
2. We feel that heav'n is now begun; It issues from the sparkling throne, From
3. And now be-fore we dwell above, We'll all surround the throne of love, And

Je-sus' ways go on; In Je-sus' ways go on; Our troubles and our
Je-sus' throne on high; From Jesus' throne on high; It comes in floods we
drink a full sup-ply; And drink a full sup-ply: Je-sus will lead his

tri - als here Will on-ly make us rich-es there, When we arrive at home.
can't contain, We drink, and drink, and drink again, And yet we still are dry.
soldiers forth To living streams of richest worth, That nev-er will run dry.

REFRAIN.

When we ar-rive at home, When we ar-rive at home, When we arrive at

home, When we ar - rive at home.

4 And now we'll shine and shout and sing,
And make the heavenly arches ring,
||: With all the saints at home :||
Come on, come on, my comrades dear,
We soon shall meet together there,
For Jesus bids us come.

Yield not to Temptation.

Words and Music by H. R. PALMER.

1. Yield not to temptation, For yielding is sin; Each vict'ry will help you
2. Shun e-vil companions; Bad language disdain; God's name hold in rev'rence,
3. To him that o'ercometh, God giveth a crown; Thro' faith we will conquer,

Some oth-er to win. Fight manfully onward, Dark passions sub-due,
Nor take it in vain. Be thoughtful and earnest, Kind-hearted and true,
Though often cast down. He who is our Saviour, Our strength will renew;

CHORUS.

Look ev-er to Je-sus, He'll carry you through. Ask the Saviour to help you,

Comfort, strengthen, and keep you, He is willing to aid you, He will carry you through.

By Permission.

61   (MUSIC ON OPPOSITE PAGE.)

1 Come, Jesus, Lord, with Holy fire,
Come, and my quickened heart inspire,
  Cleansed in thy precious blood:
Now to my soul thyself reveal,
Thy mighty working let me feel,
  Since I am born of God.

2 Let nothing now my heart divide,
Since with thee I am crucified,
  And live to God in thee:
Dead to the world and all its toys,
Its idle pomp, and fading joys,
  Jesus, my glory be.

3 Me with a quenchless thirst inspire,
A longing, infinite desire,
  And fill my craving heart:
Less than thyself, oh, do not give;
In might thyself within me live;
  Come, all thou hast and art.

4 My will be swallowed up in thee,
Light in thy light still may I see,
  In thine unclouded face:
Called the full strength of trust to prove,
Let all my quickened heart be love.
  My spotless life be praise.

62　There's a Great Day Coming.

Words and Music by W. L. THOMPSON.

1. There's a great day com-ing, A great day com-ing, There's a
2. There's a bright day com-ing, A bright day com-ing, There's a
3. There's a sad day com-ing, A sad day com-ing, There's a

great day coming by and by, When the saints and the sin-ners shall be
bright day coming by and by, But its brightness shall on-ly come to
sad day coming by and by, When the sin-ner shall hear his doom, "De-

part-ed right and left, Are you ready for that day to come?
those who love the Lord, Are you ready for that day to come?
part, I know ye not," Are you ready for that day to come?

CHORUS.

Are you ready? Are you ready? Are you ready for the Judgment day?

Are you ready? Are you ready for the Judgment day?

By permission of W. L. THOMPSON, East Liverpool, O.

HIGHWAY SONGS.

No. 2.

63   Oh yes! Oh yes!

Arr. for this Work, by J. P. WESTON.

1. My Saviour took my sins a-way, Oh yes! Oh yes! My Saviour keeps me
2. My Saviour sav'd my soul from death, Oh yes! Oh yes! My Saviour gave me
3. My Saviour he will save you too, Oh yes! Oh yes! My Saviour maketh
4. I want to know, before I go, Oh yes! Oh yes! If you love the
5. Ere since my soul was newly born, Oh yes! Oh yes! I love to help God
6. When I get on the other shore, Oh yes! Oh yes! I'll not come back to

REFRAIN.

night and day. Oh yes! Oh yes! I'm bound for the bet-ter land,
peace and rest. Oh yes! Oh yes!
all things new. Oh yes! Oh yes!
Lord or no? Oh yes! Oh yes!
work a-long. Oh yes! Oh yes!
sing any more. Oh yes! Oh yes!

Bound for the better land, Bound for the better land. Oh yes! Oh yes!

Copyright, 1886, by E. E. Nickerson.

64   All the way to Calvary.

E. E. NICKERSON.

CHORUS.

All the way to Cal-va-ry he went for me, He went for me, he went for me;

All the way to Cal-va-ry he went for me, And now he sets me free.

1. And oh, I had so many, many sins, But he took them all a-way,
2. And now my heart is full of joy and glee, And I serve him night and day,
3. My love it is rekindled, when I see The tree on which he died,

When he pardon'd me: He took them all a-way When he par-don'd me.
Since he pardon'd me, I serve him night and day, Since he par-don'd me.
When he pardon'd me: The tree on which he died, When he par-don'd me.

65   The Angels are looking on me.

Words and Music by Rev. JOHN PARKER.   Arr. for this Work, by J. P. WESTON.

1. Like Ja - cob, in his Beth-el rest, The an-gels are look-ing on me;
2. Each night I lay me down to sleep, The an-gels are look-ing on me;
3. And when I wake, new toils to meet, The an-gels are look-ing on me;
4. A pil-grim to the heav'nly land, The an-gels are look-ing on me;
5. And till I reach my home at last, The an-gels are look-ing on me;

They watch my pil-low—I am blest, The an - gels are look-ing on me.
I know I'm safe, for an-gels keep, The an - gels are look-ing on me.
God's presence makes my joy complete, The an - gels are look-ing on me.
My steps are kept by God's command, The an - gels are look-ing on me.
With ev - 'ry tear and tri - al past, The an - gels are look-ing on me.

CHORUS.

All night, all night, The an - gels are look-ing on me...

All night, all night, The an - gels are look-ing on me.....

MARY GRAHAM.   J. M. S.

1. When the voice of Je - sus calls me, And the an - gels whis-per low,
2. I have giv'n up all for Je - sus, This vain world is naught to me,
3. Just be-yond the waves of Jor - dan, Just be - yond the chill - y tide,

I will lean up - on my Saviour, In the val - ley as I go;
All its pleas-ures are for - got-ten, In re - memb'ring Cal - va - ry.
Blooms the tree of life im - mor-tal, Where the liv - ing wa-ters glide.

I will claim His precious promise, Worth to me a world of gold:—
Tho' my friends despise, for-sake me, And on me the world looks cold,
In that hap - py land of spir-its, Flowers bloom on hills of gold,

"Fear no e - vil, I'll be with you," When the pearly gates un - fold.
I've a friend who will stand by me, Till the pearly gates un - fold.
And the an - gels are in waiting, When the pearly gates un - fold.

67   "Take back the Heart."

E. E. N.   (Melody by CLARABELLE.)   E. E. N.

1. Take back the love thou hast slighted, Remember my anguish for thee ; Take back the

2. Come, ere the storm o-ver-takes you, In love I am pleading for thee ; Come, and my

freedom thou cravest, Leaving your sins all with me :   Take back the vows thou hast

Fa-ther will meet you, Come back a captive to be :   Come back in sadness and

brok-en, Fulfil them now and be free ;   Believe in the word that is writ-ten,

sor-row, Once more to suffer with me ;   I will assure thee thou'rt welcome,

Faith will give freedom to thee : ..   Gaze on the storm-cloud

The sign of the times speak my coming,   [and

Gladly I'll then set thee free : Love shall resume her dominion, Striving no more to be

flee, .. Resting 'mid strife and confusion, Leaving your burdens with me.

free, .. When on her world-weary pinion Flies back my lost one to me...

My Lord, what a Morning!

E. E. NICKERSON.

1. We shall see the great white throne, And stand be - fore it all a - lone,
2. We shall hear the trum-pet sound, 'Twill wake the na-tions under ground,
3. We shall hear him say "well done," To all who have the bat - tle won:

Wait-ing for the King to call, When the stars be - gin to fall.
Looking t'ward their Lord's right hand, When the stars be - gin to fall.
Oh, that he might claim us all, When the stars be - gin to fall.

CHORUS.

My Lord! what a morn-ing! My Lord! what a morn-ing!

My Lord! what a morn-ing! When the stars be - gin to fall.

69

For you and for me.

W. L. T.

WILL L. THOMPSON.

Very Slow. pp

1. Soft - ly and tenderly Je-sus is calling, Calling for you and for me;
2. Why should we tarry when Jesus is pleading, Pleading for you and for me?
3. Time is now fleeting, the moments are passing, Passing from you and from me;
4. Oh, for the wonderful love he has promis'd, Promis'd for you and for me;

See on the portals he's waiting and watching, Watching for you and for me.
Why should we linger and heed not his mercies, Mercies for you and for me.
Shadows are gath'ring, death beds are coming, Coming for you and for me.
Though we have sinn'd, he has mercy and pardon, Pardon for you and for me.

m CHORUS.   *cres.*

Come home,.. Come home,.. Ye who are weary, come home...
come home,   come home,

pp   ppp   *rit.*   pp

Earnestly, tenderly, Je-sus is calling, Calling, O sinner, come home!

By permission of W. L. THOMPSON, East Liverpool, O.

70   What a Gath'ring that will be.

J. H. K.

J. H. KURZENKNABE.

1. At the sounding of the trumpet, when the saints are gather'd home, We will
2. When the an-gel of the Lord proclaims that time shall be no more, We shall
3. At the great and final judgment, when the hidden comes to light, When the
4. When the golden harps are sounding, and the angel bands proclaim In tri -

greet each other by the crystal sea,   When the Lord himself from heaven to his
gather, and the sav'd and ransom'd see;   Then to meet a-gain together, on the
Lord in all his glory we shall see,   At the bidding of our Saviour, "Come, ye
umphant strains the golden jubilee,   Then to meet and join to sing the song of

crystal sea,

glo - ry bids them come, What a gath'ring of the faith-ful that will be!
bright ce - les-tial shore, What a gath'ring of the faith-ful that will be!
bless-ed, to my right," What a gath'ring of the faith-ful that will be!
Mo - ses and the Lamb, What a gath'ring of the faith-ful that will be!

CHORUS.

What a gath - - 'ring,   gath - - ring,

What a gath'ring of the lov'd ones, when we'll meet with one another, At the

What a gath - - 'ring,

sounding of the glorious jubilee! (Jubilee!) What a gath'ring, when the friends and
[all the

What a Gathering, etc. Concluded.

gath - - - 'ring,

dear ones meet each other, What a gath'ring of the faith-ful that will be!

---

71   Life for a Look.

J. M. SAWERS.   Arr. by J. P. WESTON.

I tell you, my brother, you've sinn'd quite enough; You're burden'd, don't know what to

do: Let me point you to Je-sus, Who died on the tree To

REFRAIN.

purchase salvation for you. Will you live, sinner, live, Will you look at your Saviour and

live? Now behold he entreats you, With outstretch'd arms, Take a look at him, sinner,
[and live.

2 You're now on the broad road that leads down to death;
  O, will you take warning and stop?
  O, turn to your Saviour, who pleads with you now;
  List, sinner! how gently he knocks.—*Chorus.*

3 How oft have you heard of the thrice blessed name?
  The Father, the Son, Holy Ghost:
  And should you neglect this salvation, poor soul,
  Eternally you shall be lost.—*Chorus.*

72. The Secret of the Lord.

ELLEN L. YORKE.
A Brahmin of high caste. (Chorus by R. K. C.)

R. KELSO CARTER.

1. In the se - cret of his presence, How my soul de-lights to hide;
2. When my soul is faint and thirsty, 'Neath the shad - ow of his wing,

O how pre-cious are the les-sons Which I learn at Je - sus' side!
There is cool and pleasant shel-ter, And a clear and pleasant spring,

Earth-ly cares can nev - er vex me, Neither tri - als lay me low;
And my Sav - iour rests be - side me, As we hold communion sweet;

Cho.—Safe-ly hid - ing in his presence, Guarded by his mighty sword;

For when Sa - tan comes to tempt me, To the "se - cret place" I go.
If I tried, I could not ut - ter What he says when there we meet.

Sweetly learn-ing of the se - cret, Precious se - cret of the Lord.

3 Would you like to know the sweetness
  Of the secret of the Lord?
Go and hide beneath his shadow,
  This shall then be your reward.
And whene'er you leave the silence
  Of that happy resting place,
You must mind and bear the image
  Of your Master in your face.—Cho.

4 You will surely lose the blessing
  And the fulness of your joy,
If you let dark clouds distress you
  And your inward peace destroy.
You may always be abiding,
  If you will, at Jesus' side;
In the secret of his presence
  You may every moment hide.—Cho.

73 "He never will answer me nay."

(Colossians 2: 10.)

Arr. by J. P. WESTON.

1. I shall reach those holy mansions, Where the pure hearted saints shall rest,
2. I shall walk the gold-en ci - ty, All its ra-di-ant joys to share,
3. I shall then be re - u - nit - ed With those that I lov'd on earth, Who
4. I shall then be just like Je - sus, When I look at him face to face, His

Freed from all world-ly sor '- row,   Lean-ing on his breast.
Deck'd in those robes of beau - ty,   Pure and white and fair.
bore.... their cross with pa - tience, Lean-ing on his word.
name... up - on my fore - head,   Lean-ing on his breast.

REFRAIN.

Lean-ing on his breast.   Though through the desert he lead, Or a-
Pure and white and fair.
Lean-ing on his word.
Lean-ing on his breast.

part in the mountain I pray For strength in the hour of need, "He

nev - er will answer me nay, He nev - er will answer me nay."

74. Lead me gently Home, Father.

W. L. T.
WILL L. THOMPSON.

1. Lead me gently home, Father, Lead me gently home, When life's toils are
2. Lead me gently home, Father, Lead me gently home, In life's darkest

end - ed, and parting days have come; Sin no more shall tempt me,
hours, Father, When life's troubles come, Keep my feet from wand'ring,

rit. p

Ne'er from thee I'll roam, If thou'lt only lead me, Father, Lead me gently home.
Lest from thee I roam: Lest I fall upon the wayside, Lead me gently home.

REFRAIN.

Lead me gent-ly home, Fa-ther, Lead me gent-ly,
Lead me gently home, Fa - ther, Lead me gent - ly home, Fa - ther,

By permission of W. L. THOMPSON, East Liverpool, O.

By permission of W. L. THOMPSON, East Liverpool. O.

Lead me gently Home, Father. Concluded.

Lest I fall up - on the way-side, Lead me gent - ly home.
gent-ly home.

---

75   Jesus bids you Come.

W. T. L.   *(May be sung as a Solo.)*   WILL L. THOMPSON.

1. Je - sus bids you come, Je - sus bids you come:
2. Je - sus bids you come, Je - sus bids you come:
3. Je - sus bids you come, Je - sus bids you come:
4. Je - sus bids you come, Je - sus bids you come:

Earn - est - ly for you he's call - ing, Gent - ly at thy
Wea - ry trav - 'ler, do not tar - ry, Je - sus will thy
Voic - es may not al - ways call you, "Late, too late," may
Where 'tis love and joy for - ev - er, Where we'll meet to

pp

heart he's pleading, "Come un - to me, Come un - to me."
bur - dens car - ry, Oh, will you come? Oh, will you come?
yet be - fall you, "Why will ye die?" "Why will ye die?"
part, no, nev - er, Sin - ner, come home, Oh, come, come home.

76   There is a Fountain.

ARR. by J. M. SAWERS.

Believingly.

1. There is   a fountain fill'd with blood, Drawn from our Sav-iour's veins,
2. The dy - ing thief re-joic'd to   see   That fountain in   his   day,
3. E'er since   by faith I   saw the stream Thy flowing wounds sup-ply,
4. Dear dy - ing Lamb! thy precious blood Shall nev - er lose   its   pow'r,

And sin-ners plung'd beneath the   flood, Lose all   their   guilt - y   stains.
And there have I, though vile as   he, Wash'd all   my   sins   a - way.
Re - deem-ing love has been my   theme, And shall be   till   I   die.
Till   all   the ransom'd Church of God   Are sav'd to   sin   no   more.

CHORUS.

I   do be - lieve, I   now be - lieve, That Je - sus died   for   me;

That   on   the cross   he shed his blood, From sin   to   set   me   free.

Gathering Home.

Words and Music by Rev. I. BALTZELL.

1. We'll all gather home in the morning, At the sound of the great ju-bi-lee;
2. We'll all gather home in the morning, Our blessed Re-deem-er to see;
3. We'll all gather home in the morning, On the banks of the bright jasper sea;
4. Oh, hasten thou bright, coming morning, We're waiting and longing for thee;
5. We'll all gather home in the morning, At the sound of the great ju-bi-lee;

We'll all gather home in the morn-ing, What a gath'ring that will be!
We'll meet with the true and the faith-ful, What a gath'ring that will be!
We'll meet all the pure and redeem'd ones, What a gath'ring that will be!
Thy glo - ri-ous light, earth adorning— What a morn-ing that will be!
When the captives all are re - turn-ing, What a gath'ring that will be!

CHORUS.

What a gath - 'ring, gath - 'ring, gath'ring that will be!

What a gath'ring that will be, that will be, What a gath'ring that will be, that will be!

What a gath - 'ring, gath - - 'ring,

While the angels sing, we'll all gather home, What a gath'ring that will be!

By permission. From "Heavenly Carols."—W. J. SHUEY, Dayton, Ohio.

78 The Numberless Host.

F. A. B.

F. A. BLACKMER.

1. When we enter the portals of glo - ry, And the great host of ransom'd we see,
2. When we see all the sav'd of the a - ges, Who from cruel death partings are free,
3. When we stand by the beautiful riv - er, 'Neath the shade of the life-giving tree,
4. When we look on the form that redeem'd us, And his glory and majesty see,

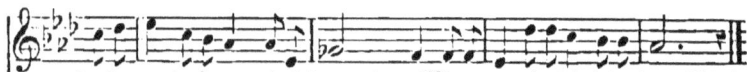

As the numberless sand of the sea-shore, What a wonderful sight that will be!
Greeting there with a heavenly greeting, What a wonderful sight that will be!
Gazing out o'er the fair land of promise, What a wonderful sight that will be!
While as King of the saints he is reigning, What a wonderful sight that will be!

CHORUS.

Numberless as the sand of the sea - - - - shore, Num-ber-less
Numberless as the sand,

as the sand of the shore: Oh, what a sight 'twill be,
as the sand of the shore;

The Numberless Host. Concluded.

When the ransom'd host we see, As numberless as the sand of the sea-shore.

---

79 ## Singing S. A. grace.

E. E. NICKERSON.

1. Be present at our ta - ble, Lord, All the way 'long it is Je - sus:

Be here and ev - 'ry-where a - dor'd, All the way 'long it is Je - sus.

CHORUS.

Je - sus, Je - sus, All the way 'long it is Je - sus, Je - sus, Je - sus:

All the way 'long it is Je - sus.

2
These mercies bless, and grant that we
All the way 'long it is Jesus,
May live to eat and drink with thee,
All the way 'long it is Jesus.
Jesus, Jesus, &c.

80   Risen with Christ.

T. E. C.   J. C. N.

1. "Buried with Christ," and rais'd with him too, What is there left for me to do?
2. "Ris-en with Christ," my glorious Head, Holiness, now thy pathway I tread;
3. Living with Christ, who "dieth no more," Following Christ, who goeth be-fore;

Simply to cease from struggling and strife, Simply to walk in "newness of life."
Beautiful thought, while walking therein, "He that is dead is freed from sin."
I am from bondage ut-ter-ly freed, Reckoning self as "dead indeed."

REFRAIN.

Glo-ry be to God! Glory be to God!

4
Living for Christ, my members I yield
Servants to God, forevermore seal'd;
"Not under law," I'm now "under grace,"
Sin is dethroned, and Christ takes its place.—*Chorus.*

81   I'm so glad.

Words arr. by E. E. N.   E. E. NICKERSON.

I know my sins are all forgiv'n, I'm so glad, And I'm on my way to heav'n, I'm so glad.
If you get there before I do, I'm so glad, Look out for me, I'm coming too, I'm so glad.

CHORUS.

I'm so glad, I'm so glad, I'm so glad there'll be no parting there.

2 Now I've got on my Gospel shoes,
  I'll run about and tell the news:
  Dear sinner, come and go with me,
  I'm bound for heaven, come with me.
3 The way is narrow, that is true;
  Just strip for the race, and you'll go thro',

The man of sin can't enter in:
  "This is the day!" why not begin.
4 Our good Lord trod the way before:
  If you lack grace, why, ask for more.
  I'm bound to go, so pray for me;
  I've shipped on board, I'm out to sea.

Walk in the Light.

Arr. by J. M. Sawers.

1. I'm a Christian, bound for glo - ry, I'm a Christian, marching on;
2. I will tell you what induced me For the bet - ter land to start;
3. When I first with Christ en-list-ed, Many said, "He'll turn a - gain:"
4. I'm a won-der un - to many, God alone the change hath wrought;

Come and hear me tell my sto - ry—All who long in sin have gone.
'Twas the Saviour's lov-ing kind - ness O - ver-come and won my heart.
But though every day re - sist - ed, In the ranks I still re - main.
Here I raise my "E - ben - e - zer," Hither by his help I'm brought.

CHORUS.

We'll walk.... in the light,........ We'll walk.... in the

we'll walk, beautiful light, we'll walk,

light,.......... • We'll walk........ in the light,..........

beautiful light, we'll walk, beautiful light,

Repeat softly.

We'll walk in the beau-ti-ful light of God, light of God.

Keep me, Lord, low down.

Arr. by J. P. W.

1. I know my sins are all for-giv'n, Carry me to the promis'd land, where
2. Poor sin-ner, you may be set free, Carry me to the promis'd land, where
3. I do re - joice for him I sing, Carry me to the promis'd land, where
4. My Sav-iour bore my sins a - way, Carry me to the promis'd land, where

pleasures never die, And I am on my way to heav'n, Car-ry me to the
pleasures never die, For you he died on Cal-va - ry, Car-ry me to the
pleasures never die, My Saviour comes, I reign with him, Car-ry me to the
pleasures never die, And I will praise him night and day, Car-ry me to the

REFRAIN.

promis'd land where pleasures never die.   Keep me, Lord, low down, till I
promis'd land where pleasures never die.
promis'd land where pleasures never die.
promis'd land where pleasures never die.

die, Oh, car-ry me to the promi-'d land, Where pleasures never die.

84   The New Song.

H. POLLARD, 1881.

Southern Melody.
As Sung by Eld. D. R. MANSFIELD.

(Arr. by F. A. BLACKMER.)

CHORUS.

Wait a lit-tle while, Then we'll sing the New Song.

Wait a lit-tle while, Then we'll sing the New Song.
Fine.

1. When the great Ju-bi-lee shall come, Then we'll sing the New Song,
2. When the long night of sin shall close, Then we'll sing the New Song,
3. When the glad shout shall rend the sky, Then we'll sing the New Song,

D.C. Chorus.

And Christ shall take his ransom'd home, Then we'll sing the New Song.
And life's fair day shall end our woes, Then we'll sing the New Song.
"O grave, where is thy vic-to-ry?" Then we'll sing the New Song.

4 When sorrow, pain and death are o'er,
  Then we'll sing the New Song,
And sighs and tears shall be no more,
  Then we'll sing the New Song.

5 When to the pearly gates we come,
  Then we'll sing the New Song;
When we have reach'd our bliss-ful home,
  Then we'll sing the New Song.

6 When we shall tread life's river brink,
  Then we'll sing the New Song,
And of those crystal waters drink,
  Then we'll sing the New Song.

7 Where all will be immortal, fair,
  There we'll sing the New Song, [wear,
When blood-wash'd robes are ours to
  Then we'll sing the New Song.

By permission.   *Copyright, 1881, by D. R. Mansfield.*

85   Love's Duet.

J. M. SAWERS.   T. WILLIAMS.

mf Andante.

1. When Jesus spoke peace to my soul, And cleans'd me from all in-bred sin, I
2. Oh! come, ye guilt-y burden'd souls, Forsake thy loathsome load of sin; Strike

promis'd God I'd follow on, The crown of vic-to - ry to win.   Since
loud and strong at mercy's door, Cry out for God to take you in: A

then his love has been my theme,   His shadow is my
bro-ken heart he'll not re-pel,   And cause your life his

And on his arm I firmly lean ;
But save your soul from death and hell,

sweet retreat,   Lead gently on, thou mighty Lord of hosts,
praise to tell,

My resting place is at his feet.
Of him who doeth all things well.

f ad lib.

Lead gently on, thou mighty Lord of hosts, Love's triumphant song, Love's triumphant
[song.

Love's Duet. Concluded.

Poco Allegretto e Animato.   *Slower.*   *a tempo.*

Oh, who can tell what joy we feel, While o'er our souls his love doth steal; His blood it

comes in soothing pow'r, And speaketh peace this very hour, To us poor mor - tal

Adagio. ad lib.

man. Oh! what love, Oh! what love, What melting, broken love.

86   Dennis. S. M.

JOHN FAWCETT.   Arr. from NAGELI.

1. Blest be.. the tie.. that binds Our hearts in Christian love;

The fel - low - ship of kin - dred minds Is like to that a - bove.

2 Before our Father's throne,
  We pour our ardent prayers ;
Our fears, our hopes, our aims are one,
  Our comforts and our cares.
3 We share our mutual woes,
  Our mutual burdens bear ;
And often for each other flows
  The sympathizing tear.

4 When we asunder part,
  It gives us inward pain ;
But we shall still be joined in heart,
  And hope to meet again.
5 This glorious hope revives
  Our courage by the way,
While each in expectation lives,
  And longs to see the day.

87   I'm Kneeling at the Cross.

Rev. J. Parker. By Permission.   S. J. Vail.

1. The blood, the blood is all my plea, Nor should a sin - ner wonder,

2. I rest, I rest, su-premely blest, With-out a care to can-ker;

3. My cup, my cup, it runneth o'er, With joy ce - les-tial brimming;

4. The blood, the blood is all my song, I have no bliss without it;

For guilty stain and stinging pain Hath tore my heart a - sun-der.

No gloomy night, my path is bright, My hope holds like an an - chor.

On wings of love I soar a - bove, His hal - le - lu - jahs hymning.

From ev - 'ry stain it makes me clean, My life and lip shall shout it.

CHORUS.

But now I'm kneeling at the cross, Washing in the crimson tide,

And cleans'd, I tar - ry at the fountain Open'd at my Saviour's side.

88 There's something more than Gold.

E. E. NICKERSON.

1. There liv'd a man in Israel's land, They call'd him Zaccheus bold; He car'd for
2. The Savior march'd in-to that town, This little man was told That Je - sus
3. He quickly ran himself to see The truth of what was told; And climbing
4. Let worldlings have their pleasures gay, And men their wealth untold; I've Je-
[sus

nei - ther God or man, But worship'd bags of gold. But worship'd bags of gold.
Christ had come that way With something more than gold. With something, &c.
up a wayside tree, 'Twas there he did behold There's something more than gold.
in my heart to-day, That's something more than gold. That's something more than
[gold.

CHORUS.

Oh yes, Oh yes, There's something more than gold. Oh yes, Oh

Oh yes, Oh yes, Oh yes,

yes,—There's something more than gold. There's something more than gold.

Oh yes,

89

A. T. SMITH.

Salvation for you.

Arr. by J. M. SAWERS.

1. O'er Co-lum-bia, from o-cean to o-cean, The Christian you al-ways will
2. We see how sin's des-o-la-tion Now threatens our land to de-
3. The out-cast, the drunkard, bring hither, And all steep'd in sin to the

see;.. Fill'd with love and a Sav-iour's de-vo-tion, Ev-'ry-
form; On... Christ, our.. "Rock and Foun-da-tion," There's
brim; May.. zeal for our Mas-ter ne'er with-er, Nor de-

where slaves of sin.. set-ting free: Our.. meetings make many as-
safe-ty a-lone from the storm. With the blood and fire ban-ner....
sire for his glo-ry grow dim. May.. we from the Ar-my ne'er

sem-ble, "Je-sus on-ly," we lift up to view; And we'll
o'er us, Though on-ly a tried faith-ful few, In the
sev-er, But.... ev-er to Je-sus prove true: And....

shout un-til Sa-tan doth tremble,—Sin-ners, there is sal-va-tion for you.
midst of our captain we'll con-quer, And tell sin-ners, sal-va-tion for you.
this be our war-cry for-ev-er,— Sin-ners, there is sal-va-tion for you.

CHORUS.

Oh, yes, there's sal-va-tion for you, Oh, yes, there's sal-va-tion for you: For

you on the cross Je - sus suf-fered, Oh, yes, there's salvation for you.

90 Prepare me.

S. CHORUS.   rall.   Fine.

Prepare me! prepare me, Lord! Prepare me to stand before thy throne.

rall.   D.S.

1. { Your garments must be white as snow, Pre-pare to meet your God! }
   { For to his throne you'll have to go; Pre-pare to meet your God! }

2 Lord, cleanse my heart, and make me
   To stand before thy throne; [pure,
   My pride, and self, and temper cure,
   To stand before thy throne.

3 My all is in the hands of God,
   If death should shake this frame!

I'll watch the path the Saviour trod,
   Till death shall shake this frame.

4 My comrades, fight with all your might,
   Soon death shall shake this frame;
   We'll live for God, and do what's right,
   Till death shall shake this frame.

91 **The journey to Canaan.**

Words from E. D. NEWTON.

E. E. NICKERSON.

1. The old Is - rael-ites knew What it was they must do, If fair Canaan they
2. Here the way is all new, As 'it o - pens to view, And behind is the
3. All my honor and wealth, And my pleasure and health, I am willing should

ev - er pos-sess'd, That they must keep in sight Of that pil - lar of light,
foaming Red Sea; So that none need to speak Of the on - ion and leek,
now be at stake; And if Christ I ob - tain, I shall think it great gain

Which then led to the pro-mis-ed rest: That their camps on the road Could not
Or to talk a - bout gar-lics to me: I'm en-gag'd in pursuit, And must
For the sac - ri-fice which I shall make: Then as loss is my gain I will

be their a - bode, But as oft as the trumpet should blow, Then all
have the good fruit, Which in Canaan's rich vallies does grow; And though
nev - er com-plain, But as long as I'm a - ble to crawl, With the

glad of the chance For a further advance, They must take up their baggage and go.
millions of foes Should rise up and oppose, I will take up my baggage and go.
res - o-lute few, Who resolve to go through, I will suf-fer the loss of my all.

Copyright, 1886, by E. E. Nickerson.

Salvation makes me Happy.

E. E. NICKERSON.

I'm glad I came to Jesus, I'm glad I am forgiv'n, I'm glad I got my sins all wash'd away;

I've the witness now within, That my soul is cleans'd from sin, And *salvation makes* [*me happy night and day.*

CHORUS.

Full salvation, full and free, I have got it, and it just suits me; I

plung'd in-to the crimson flow, The blood of Jesus cleanses me as white as snow.

2 I joined the Christian Army,
A soldier for to be,
And I'm fighting for the everlasting King:
Then let there come what may,
We are sure to win the day, [bring.
And sinners to the Saviour's feet we'll
3 And since I joined the army,
Battles I have seen, [King;
While fighting for my blessed Lord and

And with my Saviour near,
I have no cause for fear, (*sing.*
And now for Christ, my Saviour, I will
4 Now sinners come to Jesus,
And at his footstool bow, [just now;
He will pardon, cleanse, and save you all
If you will on him believe,
And his full salvation know,
With the army on to heaven you shall go!

Sing it, Hallelujah!

E. E. NICKERSON.

1. Happy day, happy day, Happy day, happy day, When Jesus, my Saviour, wash'd [my sins away;

I wept and I cried, I believ'd that he died, But how he could save me, I was not satisfied.

CHORUS.

Sing it, Hal - le - lu - jah! Sing it, Hal - le - lu - jah!

Sing it, Hal - le, — Sing it, Hal - le, — Sing it, Hal - le - lu - jah!

2 Lo, onward I move,
To a city above, [will prove;
None guesses how wondrous my journey
But this I do find,
We two are so joined, [hind.
He'll not live in glory, and leave me be-

3 I'll drink when I'm dry,
I'll drink a supply, [runs dry;
I'll drink from the fountain that never
And when I'm to die,
"Receive me," I'll cry, [why.
For Jesus hath lov'd me, I cannot tell

94   I rest upon His promise, sure.

R. E. HUDSON. By Permission.

1. Lord, I be - lieve a rest re - mains To all thy peo - ple known;
2. A rest, where all our soul's de - sire Is fix'd on things a - bove;
3. Oh! that I now the rest might know, Be - lieve, and en - 'ter in;
4. Re - move this hardness from my heart, This un - be - lief re - move;

A rest where pure en - joy-ment reigns, And thou art lov'd a - lone.
Where fear, and sin, and grief ex - pire, Cast out by per - fect love.
Now, Sav-iour, now the pow'r be - stow, And let me cease from sin.
To me the rest of faith im - part—The Sab-bath of thy love.

CHORUS.

I rest up - on his promise, sure, I come, I wait to prove

The cleansing of my heart from sin, The full - ness of his love.

From "Gems of Gospel Ssngs."

Meet me there.

Words arr. by R. H. N.   Arr. for this Work, by J. P. WESTON.

1. Just beyond there's a beauti-ful riv - er, In the re-gion of boundless de -
2. On the banks of that beau'i-ful riv - er, There will be neither sorrow nor
3. Near the banks of that beautiful riv - er, Our Re-deem-er, the Lamb, we shall
4. To the banks of that beautiful riv - er, If our garments are spotless and

light; There's no dark-ness nor cloud near that riv - er, There the
strife; We shall rest on the banks of that riv - er, And par -
see; King of kings, Lord of all he shall reign, .. And his
white, We shall go with-out sor - row or sigh - ing, We shall

CHORUS.

sun ev - er shines clear and bright. On the banks of that beau-ti - ful
take of the wa-ter of life.
brightness our glo-ry shall be.
en - ter the world of de - light.

riv - er, meet me there, meet me there; On the
meet me there. meet me there.

banks of that beau-ti-ful riv - er, Meet me there, when life's journey is o'er.

Sweetly Resting.

(Dedicated to Chaplain O. O. MoCabe.)

MARY D. JAMES.   W. WARREN BENTLEY, by per.

1. In   the rift - ed Rock I'm rest-ing, Safe-ly shelter'd I   a - bide;
2. Long pur-sued by sin and Sa - tan, Wea-ry, sad, I look'd for rest;
3. Peace, which passeth un-der-standing, Joy, the world can nev - er give,
4. In   the rift - ed Rock I'll hide me, Till the storms of life are past,

There no foes nor storms mo-lest me, While within the cleft I hide.
Then I found this heav'nly shel-ter Open'd in my Saviour's breast.
Now in Je - sus I am find-ing, In his smiles of love I   live.
All   se - cure in this blest ref - uge, Heeding not the fiercest blast.

REFRAIN.

Now I'm rest-ing, sweetly rest-ing, In the cleft once made for me;

Je - sus, blessed Rock of A - ges, I   will hide my-self in thee.

97 The half has never been told.

FRANCES RIDLEY HAVERGAL.   R. E. HUDSON. By per.

1. I know I love thee, bet-ter, Lord, Than an-y earth-ly joy;
2. I know that thou art near-er still Than an-y earth-ly throng,
3. Thou hast put glad-ness in my heart; Then may I well be glad!
4. O, Saviour, precious Saviour, mine! What will thy presence be,

For thou hast giv-en me the peace Which noth-ing can de-stroy.
And sweet-er is the thought of thee Than an-y love-ly song.
With-out the se-cret of thy love I could not but be sad.
If such a life of joy can crown Our walk on earth with thee?

CHORUS.

The half has never yet been told,   Of love so full and free;
yet been told.

The half has never yet been told,   The blood—it cleanseth me.
yet been told,   cleanseth me.

rit.

From "Gems of Gospel Songs."

98   Watching and Waiting.

" *Wait till my change come.*"—Job xiv: 14.

I. B.

I. BALTZELL, by per.

1. I will watch and wait for the morning's dawn, That will end the night of each weary [one ;

I will sing my song as the days go by, Marching onward still to my home, so nigh

CHORUS.

I am wait - - - - - ing for the dawn - - - ing,
I am waiting for the dawning of that bright and glorious day, When the

wait - - - - - - ing for the dawn - - - - ing,
storm of life is o - ver, and the mists have roll'd a - way; I am

wait - - - - ing for the dawn - - ing,
waiting for the summons that shall call me to my home, Waiting for the break of day.

2 I will watch and wait till the storm is o'er,
And a light shines out from the golden shore;
Then the Lord will say, " Weary wand'rer, come
To the land of rest, to thy blissful home."

3 I will watch and wait, for 't will not be long
Ere I strike glad hands with the blood-washed throng;
Then I'll shout and sing, while the ages roll,
Hallelujah ! Christ hath redeemed my soul !

99 Freedom.

Words and Music by J. M. SAWERS.

Arr. by J. P. W.

1. My heart was ver-y full of sin, As black as black could be; But
2. There are some peo-ple here to-night, Who look so ver-y sad; Of

Jesus whisper'd, oh, so sweet, "Dear one, I died for thee." That broke my heart; I
course, that is no wonder, For you know you've been so bad. But listen for a

then did cry With sorrow for my sins: Just then, in mercy, Je-sus came, And
moment now, For happy you can be—Just come to Je-sus as I did, And

CHORUS.

free-ly took me in. I'm hap-py, I'm hap-py, I'm happy now and
then he'll set you free.

free; I came to Je-sus as I was, And he has pardon'd me.

INDEX.

www.ingramcontent.com/pod-product-compliance
Lightning Source LLC
Chambersburg PA
CBHW021527270326
41930CB00008B/1133